KNIT LIKE A LATVIAN

50 knitting patterns for a fresh take on traditional Latvian mittens

Ieva Ozolina

www.sewandso.co.uk

CONTENTS

Techniques 114

INTRODUCTION

Mittens play an important role in Latvia's culture and history. For several centuries they were the most common type of gift in the country, and are thought by some to have magical qualities.

Mittens were most often given as wedding gifts and the act of making mittens for special occasions still continues today. Traditionally, every bride-to-be was expected to fill a "hope chest", and the most lavish chests contained several hundred pairs of handmade mittens. Mittens were also given to the family of the couple and anyone involved in organising the wedding. Nowadays, Latvian mittens, with their distinctive shape and diverse range of colours and patterns, are still a winter essential.

Most of the patterns are derived from Latvian mythology and incorporate various folk symbols (see Symbols Guide). Each knitted design has a different meaning and therefore every mitten has its own special story. Choose your favourites from this collection of 50 stylish patterns, and learn how to create your own beautiful mittens, along with coordinating fingerless gloves and wrist warmers.

SYMBOLS GUIDE

Here are some of the most common symbols featured in Latvian mitten patterns, with an explanation of their meaning.

THE SIGN OF GOD

In ancient Latvian mythology, God was not just the father of the Gods, he was the essence of them all. This symbol represents the sky, as a roof over the Earth.

THE SIGN OF MĀRA

The deity of earth and water and all the creatures within. Māra is the protector of women, especially mothers, and children. She is goddess of the Earth.

THE SIGN OF LAIMA

Goddess of destiny. Laima determined the destiny of people. The name Laima derives from the word laime, which means "happiness" or "luck". The sign is thought to bring luck.

THE SIGN OF THE STAR

The star protects from evil. The simplest form of star is a basic cross shape, created by lines crossing at right angles, which symbolises fire and the light. A cross in Latvian folklore has six or eight stars and is one of the only surviving symbols to still honour the wintertime ceremonies and celebrations.

THE SIGN OF AUSEKLIS (MORNING STAR)

The usher of the new day. Auseklis is thought to protect people from the forces of evil which roam at night.

THE SIGN OF THE SUN

The Sun is the dominant feature of God's heaven. The Sun is the goddess of fertility; patron goddess of the unlucky. The sign of the Sun is the most frequently used element in Latvian design.

THE CROSS OF MĀRA (CROSS OF CROSSES)

Related to fire, house and productivity (fertility). It guards, blesses and brings happiness.

ZALKTIS (SERPENT)

Zalktis was the guardian of wealth and well-being and therefore had to be protected and cared for. Zalktis was thought to be a sacred animal, thus had access to worldwide knowledge. It symbolises wiseness, ancient arts and sacred crafts.

TOOLS AND MATERIALS

YARN

A natural 2-ply 100% wool is recommended as the best yarn to use and is also the yarn that has been traditionally used for Latvian mittens.

NEEDLES

For mitten knitting, five double-pointed metal needles are recommended in sizes 1.5mm-2.0mm (US sizes 000-0) and length 20cm (8in). Wooden or bamboo needles are not recommended as the small sizes are too fragile and can snap easily. Magic loop technique is not recommended either, because the mitten patterns are specifically designed for knitting with five double-pointed needles and would therefore be almost impossible to follow using the magic loop technique.

OTHER USEFUL EQUIPMENT

- A pair of sharp scissors – for snipping yarn.
- A hard, see-through ruler – for measuring tension (gauge).
- A tape measure – for measuring the length of longer pieces of knitting.
- A tapestry/wool needle – blunt ended (a pointy needle will split your yarn and spoil your knitting).
- Rust-proof pins with glass heads (for visibility) – for measuring your tension squares and blocking your work.
- A blocking board or mitten blockers for blocking your work.
- Stitch markers – to mark the start of the round, or to mark a pattern repeat.
- Row counter – helpful to keep a note of how many rows you've knitted.
- Notebook and pen – as an alternative to a row counter, or to make notes of your tension or any alterations or adaptations you make to a pattern.
- Project bag – perfect for keeping your work and equipment in.

HOW TO USE THIS BOOK

BEFORE YOU BEGIN

Follow the steps below before starting to knit your mittens.

1. Read the Tools and Materials section, which specifies the type of yarn required and recommended needle size.

2. Check your tension, following the instructions below and make a note of the needle size you need to use to achieve the required tension.

3. Choose your mitten pattern and decide if you are making the full mittens, fingerless gloves or wrist warmers.

4. Choose your yarn and colours, and make sure you follow the guidelines below to work out how much yarn is required for each colour.

5. Cast on the required number of stitches as specified in your chosen pattern and work the specified cuff, following the instructions in the Basic Mitten Recipe (see Techniques).

6. Continue to work your mitten following the Basic Mitten Recipe and the chart provided.

7. Make sure you use the correct number of stitches for the thumb, as these vary between projects, and don't forget to pick up the extra "corner" stitches. Note that the thumb chart pattern may differ from the main chart pattern – if this is the case, it is charted separately.

8. Block your mittens before wearing as this will neaten up your stitches and make your patterns really stand out (see Techniques).

CHECKING YOUR TENSION (GAUGE)

Before starting your mittens you will need to knit up a tension (gauge) swatch.

Slightly looser mittens are recommended so that you can freely move your fingers inside the mittens – if your mittens are too tight and a little too small, they won't feel comfortable and won't keep your hands as warm.

Your knitted swatch will need to mirror the circular knitting of the mittens and cannot be knitted flat, as your tension will not be the same when knitting flat compared to when knitting in the round. This is because when you work stocking (stockinette) stitch in the round, only knit stitches are used, whereas when you work stocking (stockinette) stitch flat, both knit and purl stitches are used. Tension can vary when knitting these two stitches, so they can be slightly different in size and they can also use different amounts of yarn.

Several of the mitten patterns in this book include a wrist warmer variation, so it is recommended to first knit a pair of wrist warmers in order to check your tension.

HOW TO MEASURE TENSION

1. Lay your knitted wrist warmer on a flat surface. Place a see-through ruler horizontally across the top and measure 5cm (2in) across the centre of the square. Mark the beginning and end of the 5cm (2in) length with pins.

2. Do the same vertically and place pins as markers.

3. Count how many stitches and how many rows there are between the pins. This is your tension for the yarn and needles used.

For a regular size mitten knitted with 1.5mm needles, tension should be:
17 stitches and 22 rows to measure 5 x 5cm (2 x 2in).

If your stitch and row counts are the same as specified above, you can go ahead and start knitting. If you have more stitches and rows, you are knitting too tightly and your project will end up too small. You'll need to make another swatch with slightly larger needles and measure again.

If you have fewer stitches than specified, you are knitting too loosely and your project will be too big. You'll need to make another pair of wrist warmers with slightly smaller needles and measure again.

Continue to swatch with different sized needles until you achieve the correct tension stated.

If your tension testing results in a few pairs of wrist warmers that are too big or too small for your hands, then you can give them away as gifts.

The same yarn is used throughout for the mittens and their variations, so you only need to check your tension once, then make a note of the needle size you need to use to achieve the correct tension.

CALCULATING YARN REQUIREMENTS

Use the project chart as a guide for using colours – each coloured square on the chart represents each colour of yarn. The main base colour is the background colour.

For each pair of mittens or fingerless gloves, you will need: approximately 50g (175m/192yd) of the main base colour, plus 25g (87.5m/96yd) for each additional colour used. Note, for some projects, not all of the 25g (87.5m/96yd) of additional colour will be used.

For each pair of wrist warmers, you will need: approximately 25g (87.5m/96yd) of the main base colour, plus 10g (35m/39yd) for each additional colour used.

These amounts are intended as a general guide and include extra grams than required, so that you won't run out of yarn. Finished mittens usually weigh 50-100g (1¾-3½oz), fingerless gloves 50-70g (1¾-2½oz) and wrist warmers 20-30g (¾-1oz).

READING CHARTS

- Each square on the chart represents one stitch.

- Knit each stitch in the colour shown on the chart.

- Read all charts from right to left. Where one chart is provided, repeat the chart twice. Where two charts are provided, follow the right chart first, then follow the left chart.

- Where a thumb chart is provided separately, follow this for the thumb pattern. Where the thumb pattern is outlined on the main mitten chart, follow the thumb section outlined.

- For full details on the cuff method used, read the Basic Mitten Recipe (see Techniques).

- The sloping sections of the mitten and thumb charts represent the decreases (read the Basic Mitten Recipe).

- Where the chart reduces in width by one square, this indicates a decrease of one stitch for each pattern repeat; where the chart increases in width by one square, this indicates an increase of one stitch for each pattern repeat.

WINTER SUN MITTENS

Notes

Refer to Basic Mitten Recipe for full instructions.

2 colours of yarn used: base colour (white, 50g) and 1 contrast colour (dark grey, 25g).

1. Cast on 72 sts.

2. Divide equally between 4 needles on first round (18 sts per needle).

3. Start with The Notches method for the first 11 rounds (see Cuff Techniques).

4. Continue with stem and palm, following chart pattern. Read mitten chart from right to left and repeat twice.

5. When you reach the thumb round, mark thumb over 16 sts, between the red lines.

6. When you reach the base of the shaping section, start decrease rounds.

7. Work thumb over 34 sts, repeating thumb chart twice and working each additional corner stitch in background colour at the end of each repeat.

Fold here

WINTER SUN FINGERLESS GLOVES

Notes

Refer to Basic Mitten Recipe for full instructions.

2 colours of yarn used: base colour (dark grey, 50g) and 1 contrast colour (white, 25g).

1. Cast on 72 sts.

2. Divide equally between 4 needles on first round (18 sts per needle).

3. Start with the Simple Cuff method for the first 6 rounds (see Knitting Mittens: Step 2 – the Cuff).

4. Continue with stem and palm, following chart pattern. Read glove chart from right to left and repeat twice.

5. When you reach the thumb round, mark thumb over 16 sts, between the red lines.

6. Work thumb over 34 sts, repeating thumb chart twice and working each additional corner stitch in background colour at the end of each repeat.

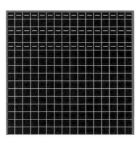

MORNING STAR MITTENS

Notes

Refer to Basic Mitten Recipe for full instructions.

2 colours of yarn used: base colour (white, 50g) and 1 contrast colour (black, 25g).

1. Cast on 72 sts.

2. Divide equally between 4 needles on first round (18 sts per needle).

3. Start with The Notches method for the first 11 rounds (see Cuff Techniques).

4. Continue with stem and palm, following chart patterns. Read each mitten chart from right to left.

5. When u reach the thumb round, mark thumb over 16 sts, between the red lines.

6. When you reach the base of the shaping section, start decrease rounds.

7. Work thumb over 34 sts, repeating thumb chart twice and working each additional corner stitch in background colour at the end of each repeat.

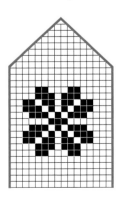

Fold here

MORNING STAR WRIST WARMERS

Notes

Refer to Basic Mitten Recipe for full instructions.

2 colours of yarn used: base colour (black, 25g) and 1 contrast colour (white, 10g).

1. Cast on 72 sts.

2. Divide equally between 4 needles on first round (18 sts per needle).

3. Start and end with (K1, P1) rib for 3 rounds.

4. Follow chart pattern for centre section. Read chart from right to left and repeat twice.

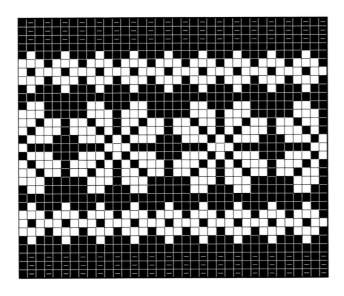

WINTER HOLIDAY MITTENS

Notes

Refer to Basic Mitten Recipe for full instructions.

3 colours of yarn used: base colour (white, 50g) and 2 contrast colours (black and red, 25g each).

1. Cast on 72 sts.

2. Divide equally between 4 needles on first round (18 sts per needle).

3. Start with The Notches method for the first 11 rounds (see Cuff Techniques).

4. Continue with stem and palm, following chart pattern. Read mitten chart from right to left and repeat twice.

5. When you reach the thumb round, mark thumb over 16 sts, between the red lines.

6. When you reach the base of the shaping section, start decrease rounds.

7. Work thumb over 34 sts, repeating thumb section twice and working each additional corner stitch in background colour at the end of each repeat.

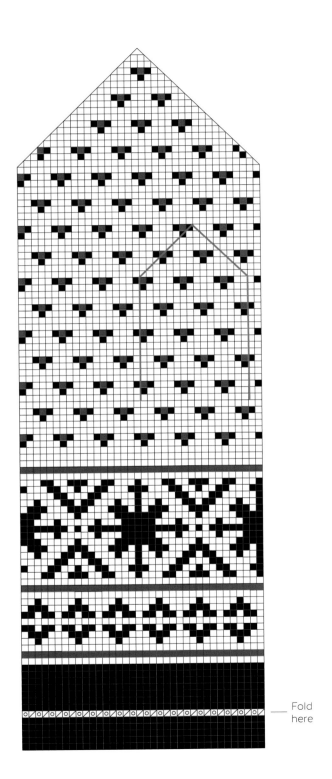

Fold here

WINTER HOLIDAY FINGERLESS GLOVES

Notes

Refer to Basic Mitten Recipe for full instructions.

3 colours of yarn used: base colour (white, 50g) and 2 contrast colours (black and red, 25g each).

1. Cast on 72 sts.

2. Divide equally between 4 needles on first round (18 sts per needle).

3. Start and end with (K1, P1) rib for 4 rounds.

4. Continue with stem and palm, following chart pattern. Read glove chart from right to left and repeat twice.

5. When you reach the thumb round, mark thumb over 16 sts, between the red lines.

6. Work thumb over 34 sts, repeating thumb chart twice and working each additional corner stitch in background colour at the end of each repeat. End with (K1, P1) rib for 4 rounds.

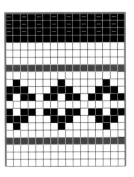

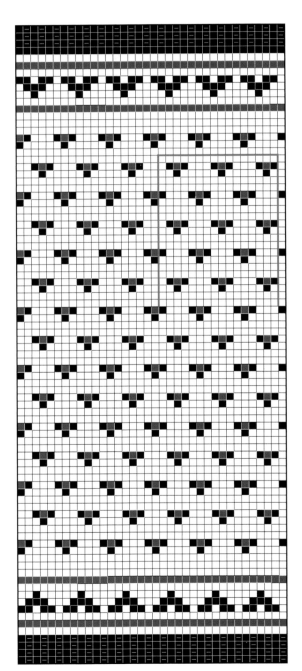

WINDMILL MITTENS

Notes

Refer to Basic Mitten Recipe for full instructions.

3 colours of yarn used: base colour (white, 50g) and 2 contrast colours (black and red, 25g each).

1. Cast on 72 sts.

2. Divide equally between 4 needles on first round (18 sts per needle).

3. Start with The Notches method for the first 11 rounds (see Cuff Techniques).

4. Work Latvian Braid where indicated on chart (see Cuff Techniques).

5. Continue with stem and palm, following chart pattern. Read mitten chart from right to left and repeat twice.

6. When you reach the thumb round, mark thumb over 16 sts, between the red lines.

7. When you reach the base of the shaping section, start decrease rounds.

8. Work thumb over 34 sts, repeating thumb section twice and working each additional corner stitch in background colour at the end of each repeat.

Latvian Braid

Fold here

WINDMILL FINGERLESS GLOVES

Notes

Refer to Basic Mitten Recipe for full instructions.

3 colours of yarn used: base colour (white, 50g) and 2 contrast colours (black and red, 25g each).

1. Cast on 72 sts.

2. Divide equally between 4 needles on first round (18 sts per needle).

3. Start and end with a Simple Cuff for 5 rounds (see Knitting Mittens: Step 2 – the Cuff).

4. Continue with stem and palm, following chart pattern. Read glove chart from right to left and repeat twice.

5. Work Latvian Braid where indicated on chart (see Cuff Techniques).

6. When you reach the thumb round, mark thumb over 16 sts, between the red lines.

7. Work thumb over 34 sts, repeating thumb chart twice and working each additional corner stitch in background colour at the end of each repeat. End with a Simple Cuff for 6 rounds.

Latviar Braid

Latviar Braid

Latviar Braid

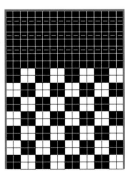

GREY NET MITTENS

Notes

Refer to Basic Mitten Recipe for full instructions.

4 colours of yarn used: base colour (grey, 50g) and 3 contrast colours (dark grey, white and red, 25g each).

1. Cast on 72 sts.

2. Divide equally between 4 needles on first round (18 sts per needle).

3. Start with The Notches method for the first 11 rounds (see Cuff Techniques).

4. Continue with stem and palm, following chart pattern. Read mitten chart from right to left and repeat twice.

5. When you reach the thumb round, mark thumb over 16 sts, between the red lines.

6. When you reach the base of the shaping section, start decrease rounds.

7. Work thumb over 34 sts, repeating thumb section twice and working each additional corner stitch in background colour at the end of each repeat.

Fold here

LUCKY SCALES MITTENS

Notes

Refer to Basic Mitten Recipe for full instructions.

4 colours of yarn used: base colour (grey, 50g) and 3 contrast colours (dark grey, white and black, 25g each).

1. Cast on 72 sts.

2. Divide equally between 4 needles on first round (18 sts per needle)

3. Start with The Notches method for the first 11 rounds (see Cuff Techniques).

4. Continue with stem and palm, following chart pattern. Read mitten chart from right to left and repeat twice.

5. Work Latvian Braid where indicated on chart (see Cuff Techniques).

6. When you reach the thumb round, mark thumb over 16 sts, between the red lines.

7. When you reach the base of the shaping section, start decrease rounds.

8. Work thumb over 34 sts, repeating thumb section twice and working each additional corner stitch in background colour at the end of each repeat.

Latvian Braid

Fold here

LITTLE HEARTS MITTENS

Notes

Refer to Basic Mitten Recipe for full instructions.

3 colours of yarn used: base colour (dark grey, 50g) and 2 contrast colours (grey and red, 25g each).

1. Cast on 68 sts.

2. Divide equally between 4 needles on first round (17 sts per needle).

3. Start with The Notches method for the first 11 rounds (see Cuff Techniques).

4. Continue with stem and palm, following chart patterns. Read each mitten chart from right to left.

5. Note that the front and back of mitten each have a separate chart.

6. Increase and decrease where indicated on charts.

7. When you reach the thumb round, mark thumb over 15 sts, between the red lines.

8. When you reach the base of the shaping section, start decrease rounds.

9. Work thumb over 32 sts, repeating thumb section twice and working each additional corner stitch in background colour at the end of each repeat.

Fold here

LITTLE HEARTS FINGERLESS GLOVES

Notes

Refer to Basic Mitten Recipe for full instructions.

3 colours of yarn used: base colour (grey, 50g) and 2 contrast colours (dark grey and red, 25g each).

1. Cast on 68 sts.

2. Divide equally between 4 needles on first round (17 sts per needle).

3. Start and end with the Simple Cuff method for 6 rounds (see Knitting Mittens: Step 2 – the Cuff).

4. Continue with stem and palm, following chart patterns. Read each glove chart from right to left.

5. Note that the front and back of glove each have a separate chart.

6. Work Latvian Braid where indicated on charts (see Cuff Techniques).

7. Increase and decrease where indicated on charts.

8. When you reach the thumb round, mark thumb over 14 sts, between the red lines.

9. Work thumb over 30 sts, repeating thumb chart twice and working each additional corner stitch in background colour at the end of each repeat. End with a Simple Cuff for 6 rounds.

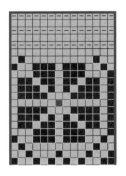

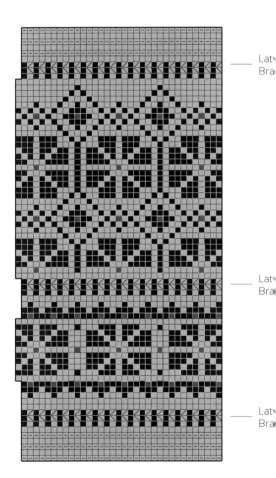

Latvian Braid

Latvian Braid

Latvian Braid

LITTLE HEARTS WRIST WARMERS

Notes

Refer to Basic Mitten Recipe for full instructions.

3 colours of yarn used: base colour (dark grey, 25g) and 2 contrast colours (grey and red, 10g each).

1. Cast on 72 sts.

2. Divide equally between 4 needles on first round (18 sts per needle).

3. Start with The Fringe method (see Cuff Techniques).

4. Follow chart pattern for centre section. Read chart from right to left and repeat twice.

5. Work Latvian Braid where indicated on chart.

6. Increase and decrease where indicated on chart.

7. End with Simple Cuff for 5 rounds (see Knitting Mittens: Step 2 – the Cuff).

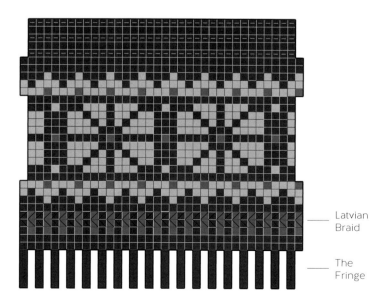

Latvian Braid

The Fringe

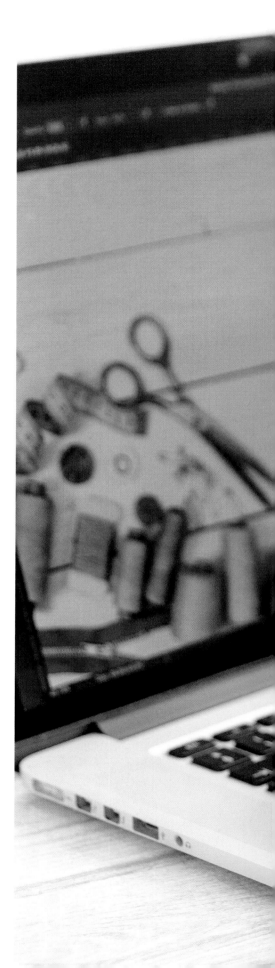

WEEKDAY MITTENS

Notes

Refer to Basic Mitten Recipe for full instructions.

2 colours of yarn used: base colour (grey, 50g) and 1 contrast colour (dark grey, 25g).

1. Cast on 72 sts.

2. Divide equally between 4 needles on first round (18 sts per needle).

3. Start with The Notches method for the first 11 rounds (see Cuff Techniques).

4. Continue with stem and palm, following chart pattern. Read mitten chart from right to left and repeat twice.

5. When you reach the thumb round, mark thumb over 16 sts, between the red lines.

6. When you reach the base of the shaping section, start decrease rounds.

7. Work thumb over 34 sts, repeating thumb section twice and working each additional corner stitch in background colour at the end of each repeat.

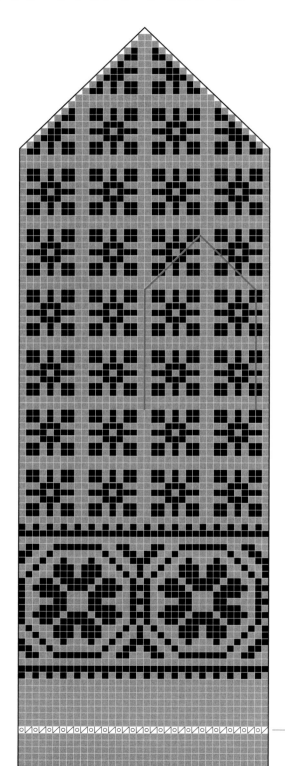

Fold here

WEEKDAY FINGERLESS GLOVES

Notes

Refer to Basic Mitten Recipe for full instructions.

2 colours of yarn used: base colour (dark grey, 50g) and 1 contrast colour (grey, 25g).

1. Cast on 72 sts.

2. Divide equally between 4 needles on first round (18 sts per needle).

3. Start with the Simple Cuff method for the first 6 rounds (see Knitting Mittens: Step 2 – the Cuff).

4. Continue with stem and palm, following chart pattern. Read glove chart from right to left and repeat twice.

5. When you reach the thumb round, mark thumb over 17 sts, between the red lines.

6. Work thumb over 36 sts, repeating thumb chart twice and working each additional corner stitch in background colour at the end of each repeat. End with Simple Cuff for 5 rounds.

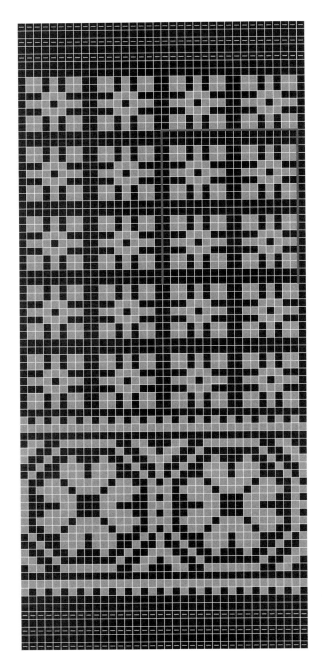

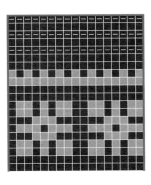

MARA MITTENS

Notes

Refer to Basic Mitten Recipe for full instructions.

3 colours of yarn used: base colour (black, 50g) and 2 contrast colours (white and red, 25g each).

1. Cast on 72 sts.

2. Divide equally between 4 needles on first round (18 sts per needle).

3. Start with The Notches method for the first 11 rounds (see Cuff Techniques).

4. Continue with stem and palm, following chart patterns. Read each mitten chart from right to left.

5. Note that the front and back of mitten each have a separate chart.

6. When you reach the thumb round, mark thumb over 16 sts, between the red lines.

7. When you reach the base of the shaping section, start decrease rounds.

8. Work thumb over 34 sts, repeating thumb section twice and working each additional corner stitch in background colour at the end of each repeat.

Fold here

MARA
FINGERLESS GLOVES

Notes

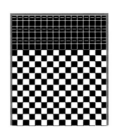

Refer to Basic Mitten Recipe for full instructions.

3 colours of yarn used: base colour (black, 50g) and 2 contrast colours (white and red, 25g each).

1. Cast on 72 sts.

2. Divide equally between 4 needles on first round (18 sts per needle).

3. Start with The Notches method for the first 7 rounds (see Cuff Techniques).

4. Continue with stem and palm, following chart patterns. Read each glove chart from right to left.

5. Note that the front and back of mitten each have a separate chart.

6. Work Latvian Braid where indicated on charts (see Cuff Techniques).

7. When you reach the thumb round, mark thumb over 16 sts, between the red lines.

8. Work thumb over 34 sts, repeating thumb chart twice and working each additional corner stitch in background colour at the end of each repeat. End with Simple Cuff for 5 rounds (see Knitting Mittens: Step 2 – the Cuff).

Lat
Bra

Lat
Bra

Lat
Bra

GREY ACORNS MITTENS

Notes

Refer to Basic Mitten Recipe for full instructions.

4 colours of yarn used: base colour (dark grey, 50g) and 3 contrast colours (grey, white and red, 25g each).

1. Cast on 72 sts.

2. Divide equally between 4 needles on first round (18 sts per needle).

3. Start with The Notches method for the first 11 rounds (see Cuff Techniques).

4. Continue with stem and palm, following chart pattern. Read mitten chart from right to left and repeat twice.

5. When you reach the thumb round, mark thumb over 16 sts, between the red lines.

6. When you reach the base of the shaping section, start decrease rounds.

7. Work thumb over 34 sts, repeating thumb section twice and working each additional corner stitch in background colour at the end of each repeat.

Fold here

GREY ACORNS FINGERLESS GLOVES

Notes

Refer to Basic Mitten Recipe for full instructions.

4 colours of yarn used: base colour (black, 50g) and 3 contrast colours (grey, white and red, 25g each).

1. Cast on 72 sts.

2. Divide equally between 4 needles on first round (18 sts per needle).

3. Start with The Notches method for the first 7 rounds (see Cuff Techniques), working just 3 rounds either side of the foldline.

4. Continue with stem and palm, following chart pattern. Read glove chart from right to left and repeat twice.

5. Work Latvian Braid where indicated on chart (see Cuff Techniques).

6. When you reach the thumb round, mark thumb over 16 sts, between the red lines.

7. Work thumb over 34 sts, repeating thumb chart twice and working each additional corner stitch in background colour at the end of each repeat. End with Simple Cuff for 5 rounds (see Knitting Mittens: Step 2 – the Cuff).

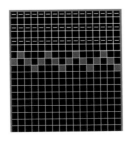

Latv
Bra

Fold
her

LITTLE DOTS MITTENS

Notes

Refer to Basic Mitten Recipe for full instructions.

4 colours of yarn used: base colour (dark grey, 50g) and 3 contrast colours (grey, white and red, 25g each).

1. Cast on 72 sts.

2. Divide equally between 4 needles on first round (18 sts per needle).

3. Start with The Notches method for the first 11 rounds (see Cuff Techniques).

4. Work Latvian Braid where indicated on chart (see Cuff Techniques).

5. Continue with stem and palm, following chart patterns. Read each mitten chart from right to left and note that the front and back of mitten each have a separate chart.

6. Decrease where indicated on charts.

7. When you reach the thumb round, mark thumb over 16 sts, between the black lines.

8. When you reach the base of the shaping section, start decrease rounds.

9. Work thumb over 34 sts, repeating thumb section twice and working each additional corner stitch in background colour at the end of each repeat.

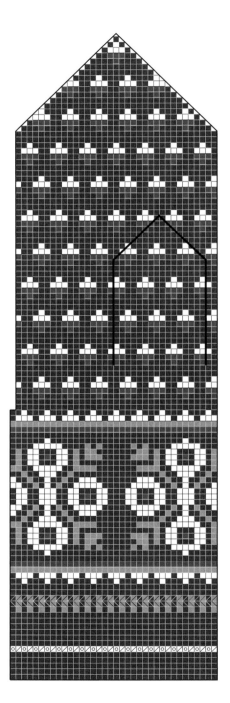

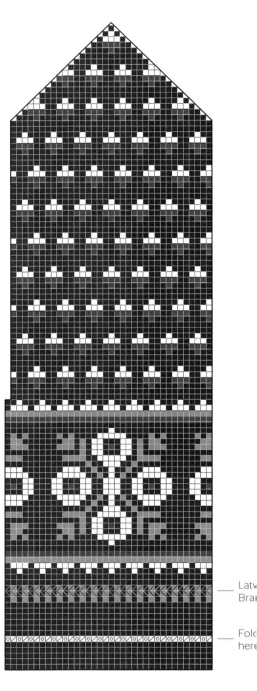

Latvian Braid

Fold here

LITTLE DOTS FINGERLESS GLOVES

Notes

Refer to Basic Mitten Recipe for full instructions.

4 colours of yarn used: base colour (dark grey, 50g) and 3 contrast colours (grey, white and red, 25g each).

1. Cast on 72 sts.

2. Divide equally between 4 needles on first round (18 sts per needle).

3. Start with the Simple Cuff method for the first 5 rounds (see Knitting Mittens: Step 2 – the Cuff).

4. Continue with stem and palm, following chart pattern. Read glove chart from right to left and repeat twice.

5. Decrease where indicated on chart.

6. When you reach the thumb round, mark thumb over 15 sts, between the black lines.

7. Work thumb over 32 sts, repeating thumb chart twice and working each additional corner stitch in background colour at the end of each repeat. End with Simple Cuff for 5 rounds.

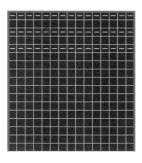

WHITE AND WISE MITTENS

Notes

Refer to Basic Mitten Recipe for full instructions.

2 colours of yarn used: base colour (white, 50g) and 1 contrast colour (blue, 25g).

1. Cast on 72 sts.

2. Divide equally between 4 needles on first round (18 sts per needle).

3. Start with the Simple Cuff method for the first 6 rounds (see Knitting Mittens: Step 2 – the Cuff).

4. Continue with stem and palm, following chart pattern. Read mitten chart from right to left and repeat twice.

5. When you reach the thumb round, mark thumb over 16 sts, between the red lines.

6. When you reach the base of the shaping section, start decrease rounds.

7. Work thumb over 34 sts, repeating thumb section twice and working each additional corner stitch in background colour at the end of each repeat.

WHITE AND WISE FINGERLESS GLOVES

Notes

Refer to Basic Mitten Recipe for full instructions.

2 colours of yarn used: base colour (blue, 50g) and 1 contrast colour (white, 25g).

1. Cast on 72 sts.

2. Divide equally between 4 needles on first round (18 sts per needle).

3. Start with (K1, P1) rib for the first 6 rounds.

4. Continue with stem and palm, following chart pattern. Read glove chart from right to left and repeat twice.

5. When you reach the thumb round, mark thumb over 16 sts, between the red lines.

6. Work thumb over 34 sts, repeating thumb chart twice and working each additional corner stitch in background colour at the end of each repeat. End with (K1, P1) rib for 6 rounds.

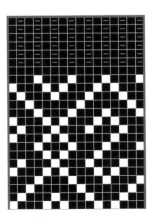

SNOWBALL MITTENS

Notes

Refer to Basic Mitten Recipe for full instructions.

2 colours of yarn used: base colour (blue, 50g) and 1 contrast colour (white, 25g).

1. Cast on 70 sts.

2. Divide between 4 needles on first round (17 sts on first and third needles, 18 sts on second and fourth needles).

3. Start with the Simple Cuff method for the first 6 rounds (see Knitting Mittens: Step 2 – the Cuff).

4. Continue with stem and palm, following chart patterns. Read each mitten chart from right to left and note that the front and back of mitten each have a separate chart.

5. When you reach the thumb round, mark thumb over 15 sts, between the red lines.

6. When you reach the base of the shaping section, start decrease rounds.

7. Work thumb over 32 sts, repeating thumb section twice and working each additional corner stitch in background colour at the end of each repeat.

SNOWBALL FINGERLESS GLOVES

Notes

Refer to Basic Mitten Recipe for full instructions.

2 colours of yarn used: base colour (white, 50g) and 1 contrast colour (blue, 25g).

1. Cast on 70 sts.

2. Divide between 4 needles on first round (17 sts on first and third needles, 18 sts on second and fourth needles).

3. Start with the Simple Cuff method for the first 6 rounds (see Knitting Mittens: Step 2 – the Cuff).

4. Continue with stem and palm, following chart patterns. Read each glove chart from right to left and note that the front and back of mitten each have a separate chart.

5. When you reach the thumb round, mark thumb over 15 sts, between the red lines.

6. Work thumb over 32 sts, repeating thumb chart twice and working each additional corner stitch in background colour at the end of each repeat. End with 5 rounds of Simple Cuff.

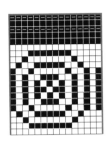

CROSSROADS MITTENS

Notes

Refer to Basic Mitten Recipe for full instructions.

3 colours of yarn used: base colour (blue, 50g) and 2 contrast colours (white and red, 25g each).

1. Cast on 72 sts.

2. Divide equally between 4 needles on first round (18 sts per needle).

3. Start with the Simple Cuff method for the first 6 rounds (see Knitting Mittens: Step 2 – the Cuff).

4. Continue with stem and palm, following chart pattern. Read mitten chart from right to left and repeat twice.

5. When you reach the thumb round, mark thumb over 16 sts, between the red lines.

6. When you reach the base of the shaping section, start decrease rounds.

7. Work thumb over 34 sts, repeating thumb section twice and working each additional corner stitch in background colour at the end of each repeat.

ORANGE SUN MITTENS

Notes

Refer to Basic Mitten Recipe for full instructions.

4 colours of yarn used: base colour (orange, 50g) and 3 contrast colours (white, blue and light orange, 25g each).

1. Cast on 68 sts.

2. Divide equally between 4 needles on first round (17 sts per needle).

3. Start with The Notches method for the first 11 rounds (see Cuff Techniques).

4. Continue with stem and palm, following chart patterns. Read each mitten chart from right to left and note that the front and back of mitten each have a separate chart.

5. Increase where indicated on charts.

6. When you reach the thumb round, mark thumb over 15 sts, between the blue lines.

7. When you reach the base of the shaping section, start decrease rounds.

8. Work thumb over 32 sts, repeating thumb section twice and working each additional corner stitch in background colour at the end of each repeat.

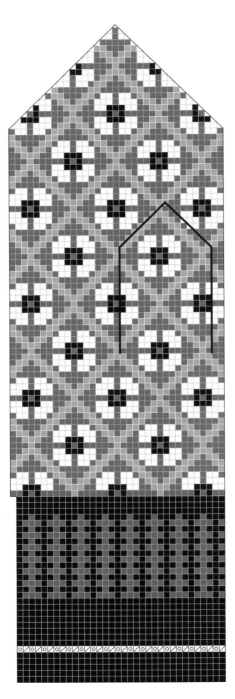

Fol
her

SNOW FLOWER MITTENS

Notes

Refer to Basic Mitten Recipe for full instructions.

5 colours of yarn used: base colour (black, 50g) and 4 contrast colours (white, blue, red and green, 25g each).

1. Cast on 64 sts.

2. Divide equally between 4 needles on first round (16 sts per needle).

3. Start with The Notches method for the first 11 rounds (see Cuff Techniques).

4. Continue with stem and palm, following chart pattern. Read mitten chart from right to left and repeat twice.

5. When you reach the thumb round, mark thumb over 14 sts, between the red lines.

6. When you reach the base of the shaping section, start decrease rounds.

7. Work thumb over 30 sts, repeating thumb section twice and working each additional corner stitch in background colour at the end of each repeat.

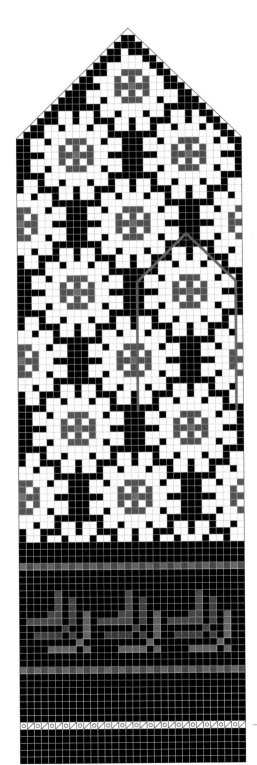

Fold here

SNOW FLOWER FINGERLESS GLOVES

Notes

Refer to Basic Mitten Recipe for full instructions.

4 colours of yarn used: base colour (black, 50g) and 3 contrast colours (white, blue and orange, 25g each).

1. Cast on 64 sts.

2. Divide equally between 4 needles on first round (16 sts per needle).

3. Start with (K1, P1) rib for the first 6 rounds.

4. Continue with stem and palm, following chart pattern. Read glove chart from right to left and repeat twice.

5. When you reach the thumb round, mark thumb over 14 sts, between the red lines.

6. Work thumb over 30 sts, repeating thumb chart twice and working each additional corner stitch in background colour at the end of each repeat. End with (K1, P1) rib for 6 rounds.

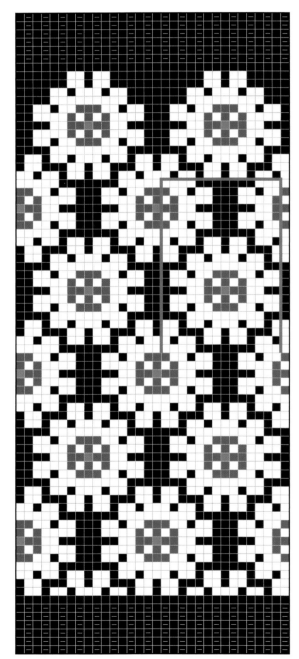

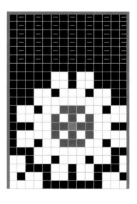

AUTUMN LEAVES MITTENS

Notes

Refer to Basic Mitten Recipe for full instructions.

5 colours of yarn used: base colour (black, 50g) and 4 contrast colours (yellow, blue, green and red, 25g each).

1. Cast on 72 sts.

2. Divide equally between 4 needles on first round (18 sts per needle).

3. Start with The Notches method for the first 11 rounds (see Cuff Techniques).

4. Continue with stem and palm, following chart pattern. Read mitten chart from right to left and repeat twice.

5. When you reach the thumb round, mark thumb over 16 sts, between the red lines.

6. When you reach the base of the shaping section, start decrease rounds.

7. Work thumb over 34 sts, repeating thumb section twice and working each additional corner stitch in background colour at the end of each repeat.

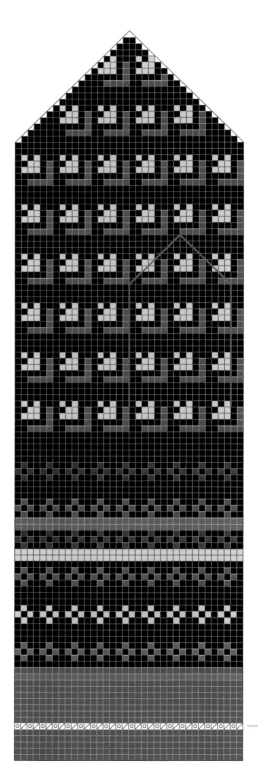

Fold here

FESTIVE MITTENS

Notes

Refer to Basic Mitten Recipe for full instructions.

6 colours of yarn used: base colour (black, 50g) and 5 contrast colours (yellow, blue, turquoise, pink and red, 25g each).

1. Cast on 84 sts.

2. Divide equally between 4 needles on first round (21 sts per needle).

3. Start with The Fringe method (see Cuff Techniques).

4. Continue with stem and palm, following chart patterns. Read each mitten chart from right to lef and note that the front and back of mitten each have a separate chart.

5. Decrease where indicated on charts.

6. When you reach the thumb round, mark thumb over 16 sts, between the white lines.

7. When you reach the base of the shaping section, start decrease rounds.

8. Work thumb over 34 sts, repeating thumb chart twice and working each additional corner stitch in background colour at the end of each repeat.

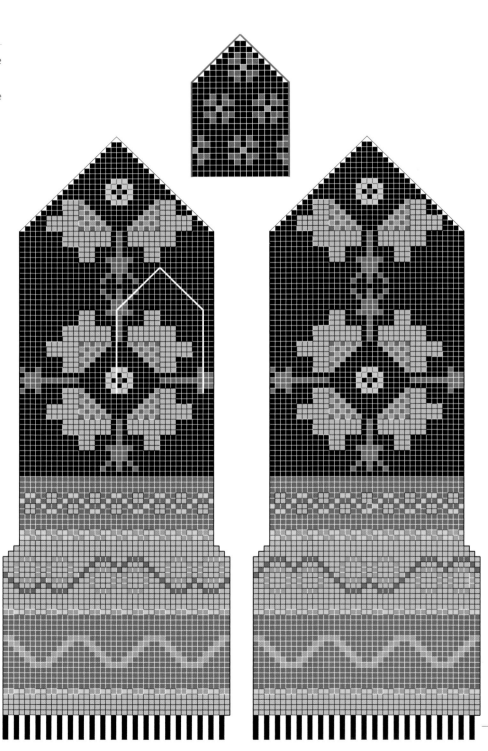

FESTIVE WRIST WARMERS

Notes

Refer to Basic Mitten Recipe for full instructions.

6 colours of yarn used: base colour (black, 25g) and 5 contrast colours (yellow, blue, turquoise, pink and red, 10g each).

1. Cast on 72 sts.

2. Divide equally between 4 needles on first round (18 sts per needle).

3. Start and end with the Simple Cuff method for 5 rounds (see Knitting Mittens: Step 2 – the Cuff).

4. Follow chart pattern for centre section. Read chart from right to left and repeat twice.

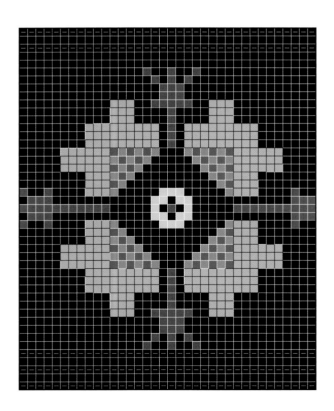

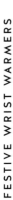

BLUE STAR MITTENS

Notes

Refer to Basic Mitten Recipe for full instructions.

6 colours of yarn used: base colour (black, 50g) and 5 contrast colours (yellow, blue, orange, green and red, 25g each).

1. Cast on 72 sts.

2. Divide equally between 4 needles on first round (18 sts per needle).

3. Start with The Notches method for the first 11 rounds (see Cuff Techniques).

4. Work Latvian Braid where indicated on chart (see Cuff Techniques).

5. Continue with stem and palm, following chart pattern. Read mitten chart from right to left and repeat twice.

6. When you reach the thumb round, mark thumb over 16 sts, between the white lines.

7. When you reach the base of the shaping section, start decrease rounds.

8. Work thumb over 34 sts, repeating thumb section twice and working each additional corner stitch in background colour at the end of each repeat.

Latvian Braid

Fold here

BLUE STAR
WRIST WARMERS

Notes

Refer to Basic Mitten Recipe for full instructions.

5 colours of yarn used: base colour (black, 25g) and 4 contrast colours (yellow, blue, green and red, 10g each).

1. Cast on 72 sts.

2. Divide equally between 4 needles on first round (18 sts per needle).

3. Start and end with the Simple Cuff method for 5 rounds in colours indicated on chart (see Knitting Mittens: Step 2 – the Cuff).

4. Follow chart pattern for centre section. Read chart from right to left and repeat twice.

MIDNIGHT FOREST MITTENS

Notes

Refer to Basic Mitten Recipe for full instructions.

5 colours of yarn used: base colour (black, 50g) and 4 contrast colours (yellow, blue, pale blue and green, 25g each).

1. Cast on 64 sts.

2. Divide equally between 4 needles on first round (16 sts per needle).

3. Start with The Notches method for the first 11 rounds (see Cuff Techniques).

4. Continue with stem and palm, following chart pattern. Read mitten chart from right to left and repeat twice.

5. When you reach the thumb round, mark thumb over 14 sts, between the white lines.

6. When you reach the base of the shaping section, start decrease rounds.

7. Work thumb over 30 sts, repeating thumb chart twice and working each additional corner stitch in background colour at the end of each repeat.

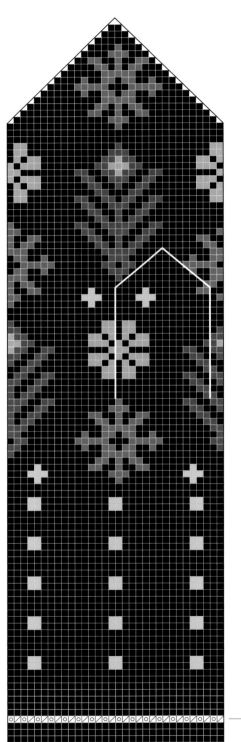

Fold here

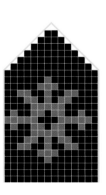

BRIGHT LIGHTS MITTENS

Notes

Refer to Basic Mitten Recipe for full instructions.

5 colours of yarn used: base colour (black, 50g) and 4 contrast colours (yellow, blue, pink and green, 25g each).

1. Cast on 72 sts.

2. Divide equally between 4 needles on first round (18 sts per needle).

3. Start with The Notches method for the first 11 rounds (see Cuff Techniques).

4. Continue with stem and palm, following chart pattern. Read mitten chart from right to left and repeat twice.

5. When you reach the thumb round, mark thumb over 16 sts, between the white lines.

6. When you reach the base of the shaping section, start decrease rounds.

7. Work thumb over 34 sts, repeating thumb section twice and working each additional corner stitch in background colour at the end of each repeat.

Fold here

PINK CROCUS MITTENS

Notes

Refer to Basic Mitten Recipe for full instructions.

3 colours of yarn used: base colour (white, 50g) and 2 contrast colours (pink and green, 25g each).

1. Cast on 64 sts.

2. Divide equally between 4 needles on first round (16 sts per needle).

3. Start with The Notches method for the first 11 rounds (see Cuff Techniques).

4. Continue with stem and palm, following chart pattern. Read mitten chart from right to left and repeat twice.

5. When you reach the thumb round, mark thumb over 14 sts, between the blue lines.

6. When you reach the base of the shaping section, start decrease rounds.

7. Work thumb over 30 sts, repeating thumb section twice and working each additional corner stitch in background colour at the end of each repeat.

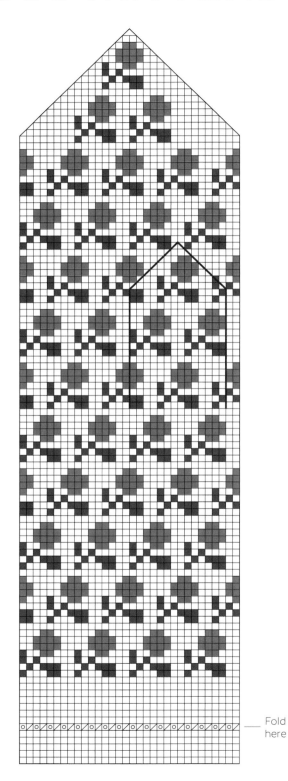

Fold here

PINK CROCUS FINGERLESS GLOVES

Notes

Refer to Basic Mitten Recipe for full instructions.

3 colours of yarn used: base colour (black, 50g) and 2 contrast colours (pink and green, 25g each).

1. Cast on 64 sts.

2. Divide equally between 4 needles on first round (16 sts per needle).

3. Start with (K1, P1) rib for the first 5 rounds.

4. Continue with stem and palm, following chart pattern. Read glove chart from right to left and repeat twice.

5. When you reach the thumb round, mark thumb over 14 sts, between the white lines.

6. Work thumb over 30 sts, repeating thumb chart twice and working each additional corner stitch in background colour at the end of each repeat. End with (K1, P1) rib for 5 rounds.

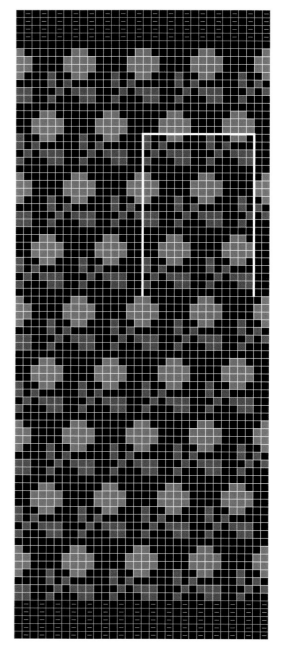

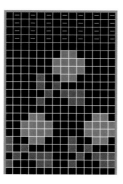

AZALEA MITTENS

Notes

Refer to Basic Mitten Recipe for full instructions.

3 colours of yarn used: base colour (white, 50g) and 2 contrast colours (pink and green, 25g each).

1. Cast on 72 sts.

2. Divide equally between 4 needles on first round (18 sts per needle).

3. Start with The Notches method for the first 11 rounds (see Cuff Techniques).

4. Continue with stem and palm, following chart pattern. Read mitten chart from right to left and repeat twice.

5. When you reach the thumb round, mark thumb over 16 sts, between the black lines.

6. When you reach the base of the shaping section, start decrease rounds.

7. Work thumb over 34 sts, repeating thumb section twice and working each additional corner stitch in background colour at the end of each repeat.

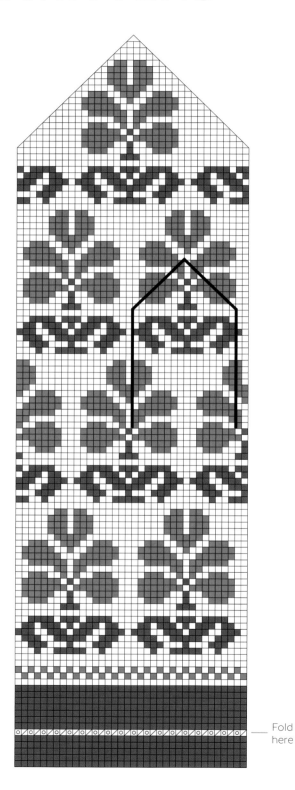

Fold here

AZALEA
FINGERLESS GLOVES

Notes

Refer to Basic Mitten Recipe for full instructions.

3 colours of yarn used: base colour (black, 50g) and 2 contrast colours (pink and green, 25g each).

1. Cast on 72 sts.

2. Divide equally between 4 needles on first round (18 sts per needle).

3. Start with (K1, P1) rib for the first 5 rounds.

4. Continue with stem and palm, following chart pattern. Read glove chart from right to left and repeat twice.

5. When you reach the thumb round, mark thumb over 16 sts, between the white lines.

6. Work thumb over 34 sts, repeating thumb chart twice and working each additional corner stitch in background colour at the end of each repeat. End with (K1, P1) rib for 5 rounds.

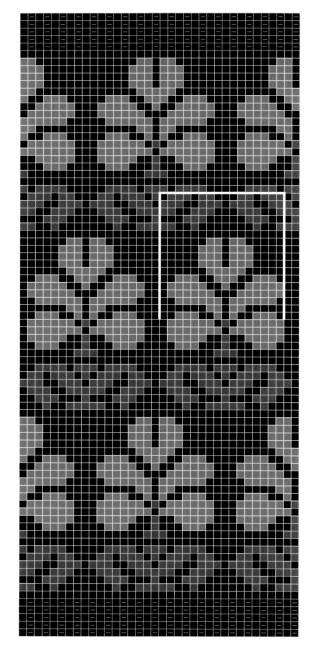

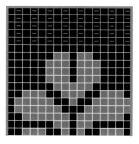

PURPLE ROSES MITTENS

Notes

Refer to Basic Mitten Recipe for full instructions.

4 colours of yarn used: base colour (black, 50g) and 3 contrast colours (purple, red and green, 25g each).

1. Cast on 72 sts.

2. Divide equally between 4 needles on first round (18 sts per needle).

3. Start with The Notches method for the first 11 rounds (see Cuff Techniques).

4. Continue with stem and palm, following chart pattern. Read mitten chart from right to left and repeat twice.

5. When you reach the thumb round, mark thumb over 16 sts, between the white lines.

6. When you reach the base of the shaping section, start decrease rounds.

7. Work thumb over 34 sts, repeating thumb section twice and working each additional corner stitch in background colour at the end of each repeat.

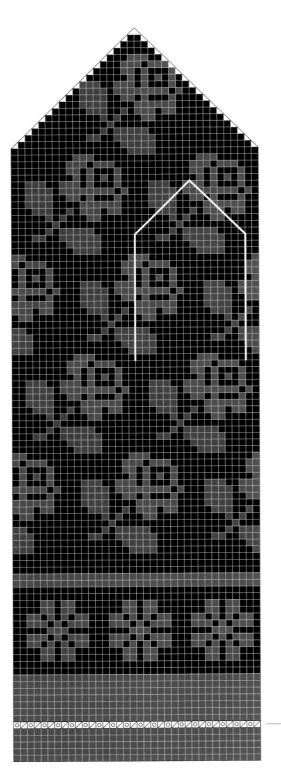

Fold here

PURPLE ROSES FINGERLESS GLOVES

Notes

Refer to Basic Mitten Recipe for full instructions.

3 colours of yarn used: base colour (black, 50g) and 2 contrast colours (purple and green, 25g each).

1. Cast on 72 sts.

2. Divide equally between 4 needles on first round (18 sts per needle).

3. Start with (K1, P1) rib for 5 rounds.

4. Continue with stem and palm, following chart pattern. Read glove chart from right to left and repeat twice.

5. When you reach the thumb round, mark thumb over 16 sts, between the red lines.

6. Work thumb over 34 sts, repeating thumb chart twice and working each additional corner stitch in background colour at the end of each repeat. End with (K1, P1) rib for 5 rounds.

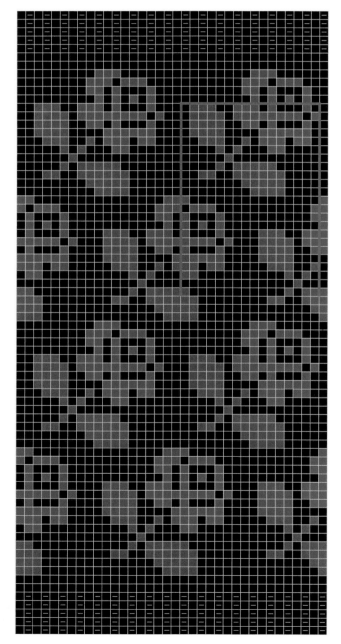

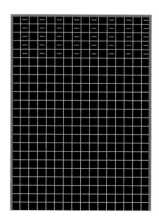

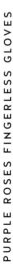

FLOWER GARDEN MITTENS

Notes

Refer to Basic Mitten Recipe for full instructions.

5 colours of yarn used: base colour (black, 50g) and 4 contrast colours (purple, red, yellow and green, 25g each).

1. Cast on 76 sts.

2. Divide equally between 4 needles on first round (19 sts per needle).

3. Start with The Notches method for the first 11 rounds (see Cuff Techniques).

4. Continue with stem and palm, following chart patterns. Read each mitten chart from right to left and decrease where indicated on chart.

5. Note that the front and back of mitten each have a separate chart.

6. When you reach the thumb round, mark thumb over 16 sts, between the white lines.

7. When you reach the base of the shaping section, start decrease rounds.

8. Work thumb over 34 sts, repeating thumb chart twice and working each additional corner stitch in background colour at the end of each repeat.

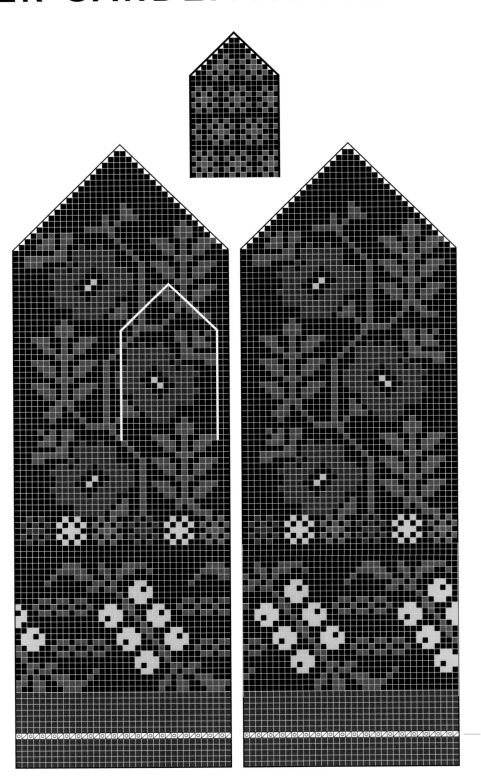

Fold here

CRANBERRIES MITTENS

Notes

Refer to Basic Mitten Recipe for full instructions.

4 colours of yarn used: base colour (black, 50g) and 3 contrast colours (red, green and brown, 25g each).

1. Cast on 72 sts.

2. Divide equally between 4 needles on first round (18 sts per needle).

3. Start with The Notches method for the first 11 rounds (see Cuff Techniques).

4. Continue with stem and palm, following chart pattern. Read mitten chart from right to left and repeat twice.

5. When you reach the thumb round, mark thumb over 16 sts, between the white lines.

6. When you reach the base of the shaping section, start decrease rounds.

7. Work thumb over 34 sts, repeating thumb section twice and working each additional corner stitch in background colour at the end of each repeat.

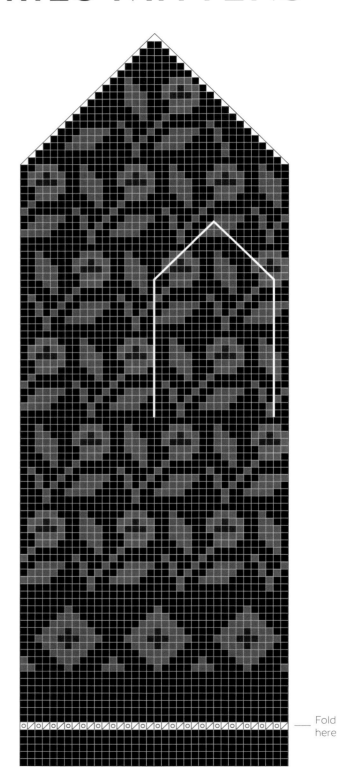

Fold here

RED ROSES MITTENS

Notes

Refer to Basic Mitten Recipe for full instructions.

4 colours of yarn used: base colour (black, 50g) and 3 contrast colours (red, green and brown, 25g each).

1. Cast on 72 sts.

2. Divide equally between 4 needles on first round (18 sts per needle).

3. Start with The Notches method for the first 11 rounds (see Cuff Techniques).

4. Continue with stem and palm, following chart pattern. Read mitten chart from right to left and repeat twice.

5. When you reach the thumb round, mark thumb over 16 sts, between the white lines.

6. When you reach the base of the shaping section, start decrease rounds.

7. Work thumb over 34 sts, repeating thumb section twice and working each additional corner stitch in background colour at the end of each repeat.

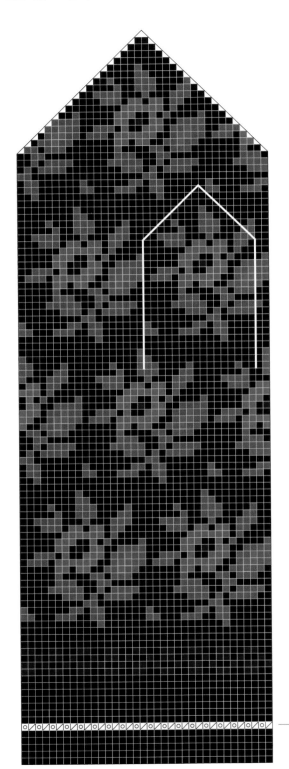

Fold here

RED ROSES
WRIST WARMERS

Notes

Refer to Basic Mitten Recipe for full instructions.

4 colours of yarn used: base colour (black, 25g) and 3 contrast colours (red, green and dark red, 10g each).

1. Cast on 72 sts.

2. Divide equally between 4 needles on first round (18 sts per needle).

3. Start and end with the Simple Cuff method for 5 rounds (see Knitting Mittens: Step 2 – the Cuff), changing colour as indicated on chart.

4. Follow chart pattern for centre section. Read chart from right to left and repeat twice.

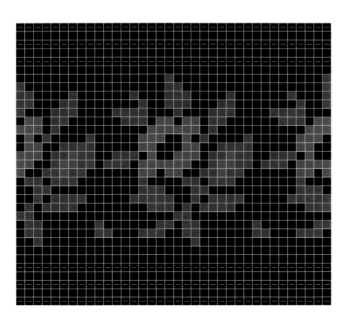

POPPY FIELD MITTENS

Notes

Refer to Basic Mitten Recipe for full instructions.

4 colours of yarn used: base colour (black, 50g) and 3 contrast colours (red, green and yellow, 25g each).

1. Cast on 72 sts.

2. Divide equally between 4 needles on first round (18 sts per needle).

3. Start with The Notches method for the first 11 rounds (see Cuff Techniques).

4. Continue with stem and palm, following chart pattern. Read mitten chart from right to left and repeat twice.

5. When you reach the thumb round, mark thumb over 16 sts, between the white lines.

6. When you reach the base of the shaping section, start decrease rounds.

7. Work thumb over 34 sts, repeating thumb section twice and working each additional corner stitch in background colour at the end of each repeat.

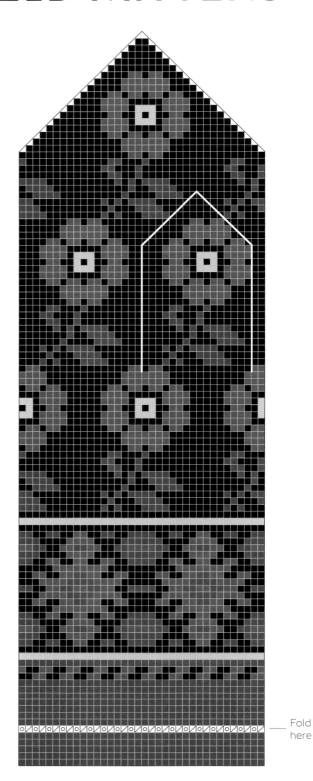

Fold here

CHRISTMAS STARS MITTENS

Notes

Refer to Basic Mitten Recipe for full instructions.

3 colours of yarn used: base colour (black, 50g) and 2 contrast colours (red and green, 25g each).

1. Cast on 72 sts.

2. Divide equally between 4 needles on first round (18 sts per needle).

3. Start with The Notches method for the first 11 rounds (see Cuff Techniques).

4. Continue with stem and palm, following chart pattern. Read mitten chart from right to left and repeat twice.

5. When you reach the thumb round, mark thumb over 16 sts, between the white lines.

6. When you reach the base of the shaping section, start decrease rounds.

7. Work thumb over 34 sts, repeating thumb section twice and working each additional corner stitch in background colour at the end of each repeat.

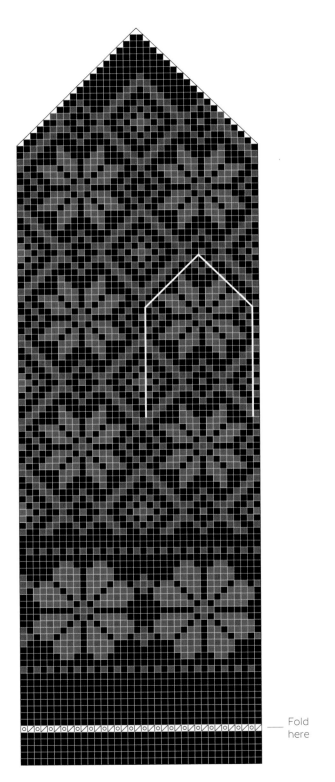

Fold here

CHRISTMAS STARS WRIST WARMERS

Notes

Refer to Basic Mitten Recipe for full instructions.

3 colours of yarn used: base colour (black, 25g) and 2 contrast colours (red and green, 10g each).

1. Cast on 72 sts.

2. Divide equally between 4 needles on first round (18 sts per needle).

3. Start and end with the Simple Cuff method for 3 rounds (see Knitting Mittens: Step 2 – the Cuff).

4. Follow chart pattern for centre section. Read chart from right to left and repeat twice.

5. Work Latvian Braid where indicated on chart (see Cuff Techniques).

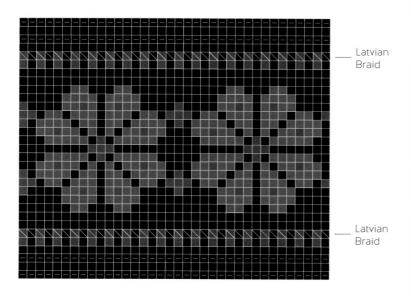

Latvian Braid

Latvian Braid

CHRISTMAS FLOWER MITTENS

Notes

Refer to Basic Mitten Recipe for full instructions.

3 colours of yarn used: base colour (black, 50g) and 2 contrast colours (red and green, 25g each).

1. Cast on 72 sts.

2. Divide equally between 4 needles on first round (18 sts per needle).

3. Start with The Notches method for the first 11 rounds (see Cuff Techniques).

4. Continue with stem and palm, following chart pattern. Read mitten chart from right to left and repeat twice.

5. Decrease where indicated on chart.

6. When you reach the thumb round, mark thumb over 15 sts, between the white lines.

7. When you reach the base of the shaping section, start decrease rounds.

8. Work thumb over 32 sts, repeating thumb chart twice and working each additional corner stitch in background colour at the end of each repeat.

Fold here

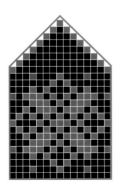

BASIC MITTEN RECIPE

GETTING STARTED

All of the mittens in this book follow the same basic knitting pattern, which consists of a cuff, stem, palm, thumb and a cast off (bind off) shaping section.

Follow the instructions below (see Knitting Mittens), alongside the colour chart of your chosen design, to create your Latvian mittens.

The mitten recipe uses symbols which are fully explained in the Knitting Symbols section. It is important to first familiarise yourself with the symbols used.

Remember to check your tension (gauge) before knitting a full mitten (see How to Use this Book).

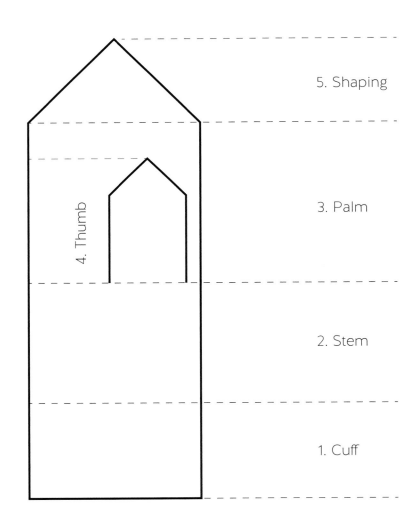

5. Shaping

3. Palm

4. Thumb

2. Stem

1. Cuff

✳ KNITTING SYMBOLS

This handy guide explains the symbols used in the charts and the mitten knitting pattern (see Knitting Mittens):

INSTRUCTIONS	SYMBOL IN CHART	SYMBOL IN MITTEN RECIPE
Knit stitch – Insert the right needle into the front of the next stitch on left needle, wrap the yarn around the right needle from back to front and pull the needle through the stitch to the front of work to create a loop on right needle. Take the original stitch off the tip of the left needle, leaving the new knit stitch on the right needle.	□	
Purl stitch – Insert the right needle into the next stitch on the left needle from the back of the stitch to the front, wrap the yarn around the right needle anti-clockwise and pull the needle through the stitch to the back of work to create a loop on right needle. Take the original stitch off the tip of the left needle, leaving the new purl stitch on the right needle.	⊟	
K2tog (knit 2 stitches together) – Insert the right needle into the next 2 stitches on left needle and knit them together as one stitch. The left stitch wraps over the right stitch, which creates a decrease of 1 stitch, slanting to the right.	◨	◹
SKPO (slip, knit, pass over) – Insert the right needle into the next stitch knitwise and slip the stitch to the right needle, without knitting it. Knit the next stitch. Insert the left needle into the slipped stitch on the right needle. Lift the slipped stitch and pass it over the knitted stitch and off the needle. The right stitch wraps over the left stitch and creates a decrease of 1 stitch, slanting to the left.		◺
Double left-slanting decrease – Insert the right needle into the next stitch knitwise and slip the stitch to the right needle, without knitting it. Knit the next 2 stitches together as one stitch. Insert the left needle into the slipped stitch on the right needle. Lift the slipped stitch and pass it over the k2tog stitches and off the needle. This creates a decrease of 2 stitches, slanting to the left.		△
Yarn over – Wrap the yarn over the needle to add an extra stitch.	⊡	

KNITTING MITTENS

STEP 1 - CAST ON

1. Using any cast-on method, cast on the total amount of the stitches onto one needle. The total amount of stitches required is specified in each pattern.

2. Divide the stitches equally over 4 double-pointed needles when working the first round of the cuff.

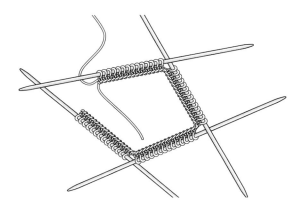

3. Tie the cast-on tail end with the working yarn, so that there is no gap between the stitches on the first and last needles.

4. Use one of the yarn tails as a marker, to mark the start of the round, and move it up every few rounds.

5. Always knit from right to left.

STEP 2 - THE CUFF

Start the cuff according to the pattern. See Cuff Techniques for instructions for "The Notches", "The Fringe" and "Latvian Braid".

To make a Simple Cuff:

1. Work 1 round in purl stitch.

2. Work 1 round in knit stitch.

Repeat last 2 rounds another 3 times, or as many time as indicated on the chart (the purl stitch round is represented by a dashed line on the chart).

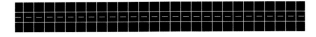

You can customise your cuff by making it longer or shorter than specified. If you find the notches cuff or the fringe cuff too advanced, you can substitute with a simple cuff.

STEP 3 - THE BODY

The rest of the mitten is completed in stocking (stockinette) stitch (knitting every round) following the pattern, reading the chart from right to left on every round.

STEP 4 - MARK THE THUMB

1. The thumb is worked over the total amount of stitches specified in each pattern.

2. The thumb is created on Needle 3 for the right hand and Needle 2 for the left hand.

3. Mark the location of the thumb with a contrast colour yarn as follows: knit the stitches for the thumb with scrap yarn (choose a strong yarn of a similar weight or thinner).

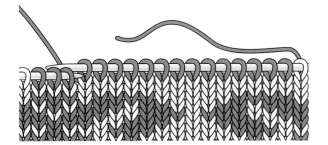

Tie the loose ends of the contrast yarn together so that it does not pull out accidentally.

4. Slide these thumb stitches back onto the left needle, and work them again with working yarn, according to your pattern.

STEP 5 – FINISH THE BODY

To finish the body, work in stocking (stockinette) stitch according to the pattern, reading the chart from right to left on every round, until the decrease round is reached.

STEP 6 – DECREASE

The decrease of a Latvian mitten is made in the form of a triangle.

1. One decrease round reduces 4 stitches in total.

2. You will decrease at the beginning and at the end of alternate needles: at the beginning of Needle 1 and Needle 3; at the end of Needle 2 and Needle 4. This makes it easier to keep track of your decreases.

3. At the beginning of Needle 1 and Needle 3: knit 1, slip 1, knit 1, pass slipped stitch over ($\triangle$), knit the remaining stitches.

4. At the ends of Needle 2 and Needle 4: knit to the last 3 stitches, knit 2 stitches together ($\triangle$), knit 1.

5. Continue decreasing in this way until you have only 2 stitches left on each needle.

6. Using tapestry/wool needle, take the thread through the stitches and pull the yarn tail through to the wrong side and secure.

STEP 7 – THE THUMB

1. Use one needle to pick up the stitches directly above the scrap yarn – picking up the right leg of each stitch and working from right to left. Use a second needle to pick up the stitches directly below the scrap yarn in exactly the same way.

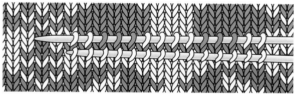

2. Pick up 1 stitch at each opposite "corner" of the thumbhole between the lower and upper needles. Use lifted strand stitch by inserting the left needle under the loop of yarn, from the back, and slipping it onto the right needle.

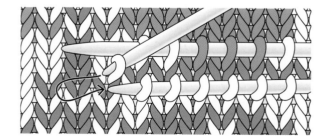

3. Rearrange the stitches so that they are evenly distributed on four needles. If the stitch count is not divisible by 4, make sure that the extra 2 stitches picked up at the corners are on Needles 1 and 3, or on Needles 2 and 4.

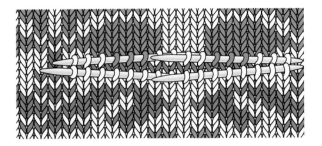

4. Rejoin main colour yarn – join it to the stitch that sits to the right of the first stitch.

5. Remove the scrap yarn used to mark the thumb.

6. In the first round, twist the picked up corner stitches when knitting them to avoid making holes, by inserting the right needle purlwise into the front of the corner stitch, then manoeuvre the right needle over the tip of the left needle (don't let the stitch fall off) so that it sits behind the left needle (needles are now in the usual position for knit stitch).

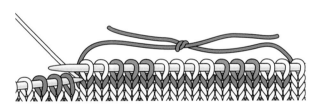

7. Knit straight following the chart, until thumb measures the required length or until the base of your thumbnail is reached. Note the following for the thumb knitting:

- In most mittens, the thumb chart is outlined in red on the main mitten chart. These thumbs blend seamlessly into the mitten.

- For others, the thumb chart pattern is a contrast pattern and will appear as a separate chart.

- Also, for some mittens, the pattern on the back of the thumb is different to the front of the thumb.

- The additional corner stitches picked up for the thumb are not included in the chart for any thumb pattern. For these stitches you knit them in background colour – hence you treat the thumb front and thumb back as two separate patterns, separated by a column of background stitches.

STEP 8 - THUMB DECREASE

1. Thumb decreases are worked in the same way as mitten decreases – working a decrease at the beginning and at the end of alternate needles.

2. At the beginning of a needle decrease (Needles 1 and 3): knit 1, slip 1, knit 1, pass slipped stitch over (△).

3. At the end of a needle decrease (Needles 2 and 4): knit 2 stitches together (△), knit 1.

4. Continue decreasing until there are 10 stitches in total – 5 stitches left on front side needles and 5 stitches left on back side needles (10 stitches over four needles).

5. Divide all stitches between two needles – 5 stitches on one needle and 5 on another – and continue knitting with third needle.

6. Knit the last round as follows: *slip 1, knit 2 together, pass slipped stitch over (△), knit 2 stitches together (△); repeat from * once more.

7. Cut yarn and pull through stitches. Turn the thumb inside out, pull the yarn tail through to the wrong side and secure. If there are holes at the base of the thumb, use the yarn tail there to tighten it up.

FINGERLESS GLOVES

To make fingerless gloves, repeat Steps 1-5 from Knitting Mittens.

To finish the glove on the last round, use the free needle to cast off (bind off) the stitches on the first needle until one stitch remains. Drop the free needle and use the needle with the one remaining stitch to cast off (bind off) the stitches on the next needle to the last stitch. Continue in this way to the last stitch on the last needle and fasten off this stitch. Use the tail end of yarn to close up the gap between the first and last stitches.

Work Step 7 – The Thumb from Knitting Mittens, then cast off (bind off) and finish the thumb the same way as given for the hand section.

WRIST WARMERS

To make wrist warmers, repeat Steps 1-4 from Knitting Mittens.

To finish the wrist warmers on the last round, use the free needle to cast off (bind off) the stitches on the first needle until one stitch remains. Drop the free needle and use the needle with the one remaining stitch to cast off (bind off) the stitches on the next needle to the last stitch. Continue in this way to the last stitch on the last needle and fasten off this stitch. Use the tail end of yarn to close up the gap between the first and last stitches.

CUFF TECHNIQUES

THE NOTCHES

1. Work 5 rounds (or as many rounds as stated in the pattern) in knit stitch.

2. Knit 1 round according to the instructions below:

[K2tog, yo] to the end (△).

Note that the "yo" creates a hole in your knitting. This round is the foldline.

3. Work a further 5 rounds (or as many rounds as stated in the pattern) in knit stitch, as you did in Step 1.

4. Fold your knitting at the foldline, bringing the cast-on edge up at the back of your needles to meet the working edge.

5. For the next round, knit together one stitch from the left needle with one stitch from the cast-on edge of the knitting and making sure that these stitches are in line with each other. To do this, insert the right needle into the corresponding stitch along the cast-on edge.

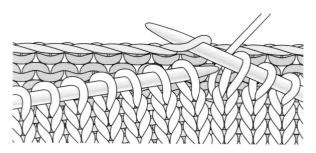

Place this stitch on the tip of the left needle. Knit this stitch and the next stitch together as one stitch. Repeat this process for the remainder of the round, to complete the notches cuff.

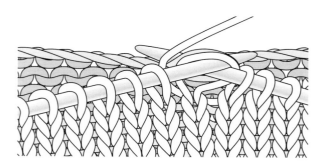

The notches cuff is represented on a chart as follows:

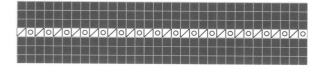

THE FRINGE

1. Work the first row in purl stitch and divide your stitches equally between 4 needles.

2. Hold your index finger behind the needles and wind yarn 3 times, loosely, around the index finger from front to back. The wrong side of the knitting is facing you.

3. Insert right needle into the next stitch on the left needle, knitwise, then insert right needle under the wrapped yarn around finger, purlwise.

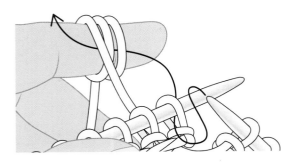

4. Pull the wrapped yarn through the stitch on left needle and very carefully remove your finger. You now have the 3 loops of yarn on your right needle. Take care not to pull the working yarn, otherwise you will pull out the loops just made. The loops will sit behind the needles, and note that the side of knitting facing you is the wrong side. Try to keep your loops the same size for every stitch.

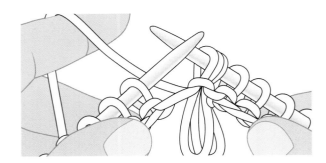

5. Work in alternate colours, if desired.

6. When all of the fringe is knitted, turn the knitting to the right side.

7. Knit 1 round in knit stitch, then follow the pattern chart. You can gently pull down on each loop after the knit round.

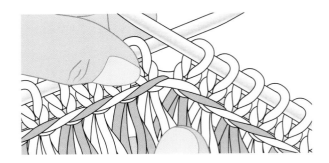

The fringe cuff is represented on a chart as follows:

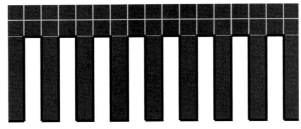

LATVIAN BRAID

Knitted using two colours, over two rounds.

1. Choose one colour for A and another for B.

2. Knit first round as follows: *k1 with A, k1 with B; repeat from * to the end of round.

3. Bring both yarns forward between needles to the front of the work.

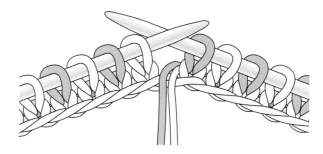

4. Purl second round in the same colour sequence: *p1 with A, p1 with B; repeat from * to end of round and each time, bring the next colour over the yarn you have just knitted with, to create the braiding effect.

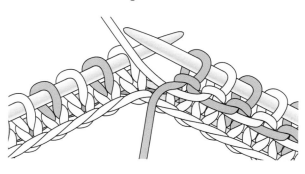

5. Take both yarns between needles to back of work. Knit one row in the base colour of the pattern and then continue to follow the chart pattern.

6. To create a double Latvian Braid, repeat Step 4 once more, but each time passing the new yarn **under** the yarn you have just knitted with.

The Latvian Braid is represented on a chart as follows:

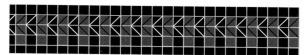

STRANDING YARN

When you are working with one or more strands of yarn at a time, it is important to keep the balls of yarn separated so that they do not become tangled. It helps if you can place one ball of yarn on your right and one ball of yarn on your left.

Always carry the yarn not being used loosely across the back of your work until you need it next, and don't pull it too tightly, otherwise your knitting will pucker.

When changing colour, always choose one colour that will feed in to your knitting above the other colour (from the top) and feed the other colour in from the bottom. If you maintain this order throughout your knitting, your fairisle patterning will look uniform and neat.

BLOCKING YOUR PROJECTS

Once you have finished your mittens, fingerless gloves or wrist warmers, it is recommended to block them, to even out the stitches. Spray one side of knitting with cold water until wet, but not saturated. Gently press the water into the stitches with your hands, then pin flat to dry. Repeat for the opposite side. If you feel that your mittens need stretching slightly to fit, pin to the size desired (or use a mitten blocker) and leave to dry.

✳ BASIC KNITTING TECHNIQUES

CASTING ON

  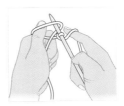 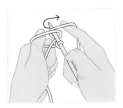 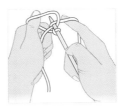

CASTING OFF (BINDING OFF)

  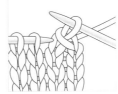

KNIT STITCH – ENGLISH METHOD

KNIT STITCH – CONTINENTAL METHOD

PURL STITCH – ENGLISH METHOD

PURL STITCH - CONTINENTAL METHOD

DECREASING - K2TOG - KNIT TWO STITCHES TOGETHER

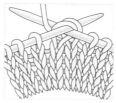

DECREASING - SKPO - SLIP ONE STITCH, KNIT ONE STITCH, PASS SLIPPED STITCH OVER THE KNITTED STITCH

INCREASING - M1 - MAKE ONE STITCH

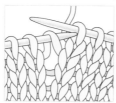 

INCREASING - KFB - KNIT INTO FRONT AND BACK OF STITCH

ABOUT THE AUTHOR

Ieva Ozolina is the founder and creator of the Hobbywool and the "Knit Like a Latvian" kits. Ieva started knitting when she was 14 and has been passionate about knitting ever since. In 2009 she started her own knitting and yarn company called "Hobbywool".

Ieva has taken her "Knit Like a Latvian" knitting kits to over 30 international fairs and exhibitions to spread her love for Latvian mittens all over the world.

Ieva lives in Riga, Latvia, and runs her yarn shop in the Old Town of Riga together with her husband Maris.

THANK YOU

First of all I want to thank all Latvian women, who have knitted mittens for centuries, keeping traditions alive and leaving us with the most beautiful heritage of mitten patterns.

I want to thank Sarah Callard, Commissioning Editor at F&W Media, who offered me the great opportunity to write this book.

Thanks to Dr.hist Aija Jansone, whose books and wide knowledge about Latvian mittens inspired me to create my own "Knit Like a Latvian" mitten knitting kits.

Thanks to Betija Markusa, who has been my biggest help in writing and creating this book.

And BIG thanks to my dear family: my husband Maris for his tremendous support and keeping me patient & calm; my son Jekabs for his help in meetings and translation; my daughter Eliza for encouragement; my granddaughter Katrina for showing interest in my work and giving me hope that my work will be continued; my French bulldog BIMO for guarding my yarn balls, playing with them and making me smile; and thanks to each and every one of you who bought this book. With all of my heart I hope that your mittens will turn out beautiful!

SUPPLIERS

Hobbywool 2-ply 100% wool yarns are made in Latvia and are the perfect choice for mittens knitting. All yarns are made only from natural fibres and at Hobbywool you will find a wide range of colours – from earth tones to bright colours.

All Hobbywool yarns and knitting tools can be purchased direct from:

www.hobbywool.com

INDEX

A SEWANDSO BOOK
© F&W Media International, Ltd 2018

SewandSo is an imprint of F&W Media International, Ltd
Pynes Hill Court, Pynes Hill, Exeter, EX2 5AZ, UK

F&W Media International, Ltd is a subsidiary of F+W Media, Inc
10151 Carver Road, Suite #200, Blue Ash, OH 45242, USA

Text and Designs © Ieva Ozolina 2018
Layout and Photography © F&W Media International, Ltd 2018

First published in the UK and USA in 2018

A catalogue record for this book is available from the British Library.

ISBN-13: 978-1-4463-0672-7 paperback
SRN: R6806 paperback

ISBN-13: 978-1-4463-7640-9 PDF
SRN: R6709 PDF

ISBN-13: 978-1-4463-7639-3 EPUB
SRN: R6708 EPUB

Printed in the U.S.A. by LSC Communications for:
F&W Media International, Ltd
Pynes Hill Court, Pynes Hill, Exeter, EX2 5AZ, UK

10 9 8 7 6 5

Content Director: Ame Verso
Acquisitions Editor: Sarah Callard
Managing Editor: Jeni Hennah
Project Editor: Lynne Rowe
Proofreader: Cheryl Brown
Design Manager: Lorraine Inglis
Designer: Sam Staddon
Illustrator: Kuo Kang Chen
Photographer: Jason Jenkins
Production Manager: Beverley Richardson

F&W Media publishes high quality books on a wide range of subjects.
For more great book ideas visit: www.sewandso.co.uk

Layout of the digital edition of this book may vary depending on reader hardware and display settings.

Eagan Press Handbook Series

Sweeteners: Nutritive

R. J. Alexander

 eagan press
St. Paul, Minnesota, USA

Cover: Sugar beet, Don Lilleboe/The Sugarbeet Grower Magazine; sugar crystal, ©1997 by PhotoDisc, Inc.; laboratory products courtesy of the Department of Food Science and Nutrition, University of Minnesota, St. Paul.

Library of Congress Catalog Card Number: 98-71600
International Standard Book Number: 0-913250-95-3

©1998 by the American Association of Cereal Chemists, Inc.

Printed in the United States of America on acid-free paper

American Association of Cereal Chemists
3340 Pilot Knob Road
St. Paul, Minnesota 55121-2097, USA